POETRY

Poetry

John Maclennan

Edited and compiled by Virginia Bowen

Illustrated by Sarah Clement

REGENT COLLEGE PUBLISHING

Vancouver, British Columbia

Regent College Publishing
5800 University Boulevard
Vancouver, BC V6T 2E4 Canada

Regent College Publishing is an imprint of the Regent Bookstore (RegentBookstore.com). Views expressed in works published by Regent College Publishing are those of the author and do not necessarily represent the official position of Regent College (Regent-College.edu).

ISBN 978-1-57383-567-1

Cataloguing in Publication information is available from Library and Archives Canada.

POETRY

I wonder about things day after day,

turning pages in my mind.

They reveal nothing that I did not already know,

and in everything, I am left far behind.

Thank you, my God, my Saviour

Leading me into fields unknown

Where I can grow and prosper

and find the way back to fields that were sown.

You have led me all the days of my life.

From beginning to end, it is quite a story

Where sin and destruction thrived and grew.

Regard for You faded,

Your will forgotten,

While I sowed a field of thorns of strange hue.

I thought I saw you standing,

weeping in the rain.

Summer comes tomorrow

And will wipe away the pain.

Greet it with a blessing.

Meet it with a smile.

Shout a hallelujah.

It means you've gone another mile.

Road's end comes to meet us,

laughing in the dark.

That will be a day

That lights another spark.

We write about our strivings

and hope to succeed.

And we leave the result

to Him who waters the seed.

I have understood now

that we can't play a game

When it comes to deciding

The fate of our race.

The dark days slip away

into an endless night.

How does one day pass

slipping from sight?

Would that they came back to us,

shining and new,

Showing us everything we wanted to do.

But time passes onward,

relentless and slow,

Ending our dreams

and destroying our hope.

But light shines from the heavens,

resplendent and bright,

and destroys all the shadows and darkness of night

Till we come to a place where we see and believe

that what was lost we can now retrieve.

Talk to me about what you have seen,

the earth and its beauty

and all that has been.

Speak softly and sweetly

and in gentle tones.

Don't alarm me

or leave me ever alone.

What do You want to say to me?

Something I understand

Why the world keeps turning

while my fate is in my hand.

You know the reason this is so,

for You created it all.

You showed me the way it was

a long time ago.

And how Your love turned it round,

so it found a place to go.

So is the life of mankind,

evermore twisting and turning,

Trying to find a way to eternity

and to be there when You call.

But this is the mystery of life.

Sense is wrapped up in nonsense

and can never

be unwrapped at all.

What happened yesterday will happen today.

Each day tells its story in a new way.

I have learnt that we never learn anything in life

but are pulled by distant forces forever in strife.

I wish I knew the beginning and end

and what lay between, perhaps,

but that is too much to ask for.

So, we are left with this moment

to savour and enjoy

till our time runs out.

Hope is something we long for,

budding and growing unseen,

Awaiting the time of its moment

to reveal its blazing sheen.

The earth is a cauldron,

Swirling and deep.

Whoever finds his way through it,

a harvest he does reap.

Its answer I know not.

Its questions are deep.

What remains to be said

is lost when I sleep.

Every day brings sorrow, grief, or pain.

Days, why do you wrack me with suffering,

all to no gain?

I learn from them as they go floating by.

I learn and discover the secret of why.

Light dawns on the path to truth.

And I wish I had never been there

or tasted the lies of youth.

It was bitter to take

and harder to swallow.

But I knew the end that would follow.

It led me on a way past a path unending

to the riches of the Homeland of Truth.

The Heart knows the reasons

that the mind cannot fathom.

God knows our heart

and caresses it gently.

All his truth is poured out there

and there understood.

Let us stand in awe of its greatness,

guiding and leading us all of our lives.

Thank you, God, for giving us

This heart of gold

that knows and feels

All You tell it

and reaches ever upward

For all that You know.

I thought about you yesterday

when the sun shone in the sky.

All those days that heaven made

that have long passed by.

I hope to greet you tomorrow

when the sun is red again.

All those days

like yesterday

will come flooding back again.

You came to me out of the darkness

and filled my world with light.

You came to reassure me

and blot out forever the night.

Aphrodite in a cupboard

Bare and polished, honed and dry

We could make our life on airships

We could make them fly.

Twelve noon strikes the note of doom

Each stroke resonates so firmly.

Each stroke hammers on the tomb.

Life is vacant. Life is empty,

Fitted for eternal note,

Constancy in seeing plenty,

And being savaged by a quote.

Epithalamion of tears,

Turgid river, play of words,

Softly, softly cross my heart.

Whisper words that echo fears.

I would like to know you, God,

to see into your heart,

To feel your hand on mine

And know from where to start.

The world turns slowly.

Onward and on it goes,

Spanning the history of our lives.

Much in that story is forgotten.

But some we remember

and cherish dear,

Holding them close to our heart.

The day that is now

soon will be gone

Like all of our yesterdays done.

So, turn the days over carefully

and live them fully

Until all are gone.

Creation is an act of the spirit

That comes and makes things whole.

Everything comes from it,

From our own soul.

I woke and called it yesterday

as trumpets brayed retreat.

I heard the sound of battle songs

and knew it was defeat.

Fire over fire rained on us

and shook the very earth.

We tasted blood and sweat and tears

and came to new birth.

Advance! they cried

and urged us on.

Retreat our souls would say.

Life's very essence was poured out

at the dawning of the day.

Goodbye to battle sounds and storms.

Goodbye to fiery dread.

We walk on earth a chosen race

who bled and bled and bled.

And now I come to peaceful times

when the battle reigns no more,

To armchair ease and cups of tea

and steps behind the door.

An eager tomorrow awaits me,

Spinning out of time.

Yesterday's shadows encumber it.

They will never fall into line.

But we have a Creator who laughs,

Who bids all these things adieu.

They shall never come near us,

Hurt us, or block out our view.

I was out on a journey one day,

crossing the world to and fro.

The sky changed patterns above me,

and I knew there was nowhere to go.

Then You suddenly appeared before me,

and all the world had suddenly a tilt.

You had unwrapped the meaning of life,

and I knew my life would not wilt.

Echoes of what You said then

have followed me all of my days.

And the doors You opened before me

have led me to glory and praise.

Happiness comes

Stolen from yesterday,

Illuminating the sun

and leading the way.

I will bear the blows of fortune.

I will take what heaven sends.

I will wend my way through life

Till I reach the end of ends.

Tomorrow will rise sun blest,

All those yesterdays forgot.

What has been will be no more,

What was then and what was not.

I will stride the path of hope

till at last it leads me home.

I will know the fortune finished.

Time at last to cease to roam.

I know a wonderful person

whose face often shows a smile,

Who understands all my uncertainties

and knows how to let things go for a while.

A woman dances in vibrant red.

Her hand lifted, cleaving the air.

Every movement expresses emotion,

but her face has an air of despair.

Behind her, the audience watches,

serious and wrapped in their thoughts,

Gazing steadfastly onwards,

awaiting an answer to prayer.

How shall the old greet the young?

Whispering across the years,

How can we meet and understand

the changes that our lives steer?

These questions defy understanding,

Riddles that are open and show

No one has found the answer

or found a place to go.

Why do I bother to ask them?

Questions that don't have an answer

I think I'm understanding

something I will finally know.

One year follows another.

The years pile up,

Echoing from one to another,

Teaching undying songs.

What can you teach me, years?

What can you tell me, life?

Read me the story of man.

Whisper his tale of strife.

Out of your womb comes learning.

Out of your rest comes joy

As we tread the steps of our lifetime,

As we walk in the vale destroyed.

Yesterday everything happened.

Nothing was left unsaid.

What you said broke my heart in pieces

and left me alone, the undead.

You taught me a little of life.

You helped me along the way.

Now you have gone forever

and left me with nothing to say.

I'll always remember our friendship

and treasure the times we had.

Thank you for making it easy.

Thank you for ending the bad.

When You come, You bring endless grace

to help us along the road of life

Where pitfalls everywhere abound.

You show us new life.

Thank you for all that You do,

patiently working to open my mind,

So that I can understand your purposes

and find a way out of a road that is blind.

The beauty of a flower

mirrors the beauty of a tree.

The beauty of its face

mirrors that of you and me.

Rain, you fill the ground and soak

the way for spring time blooms,

Bringing new life in hope.

I'll love forever the sound you make,

Plinking and dappling on leaf and tree,

Refreshing and waking the world to life,

Showing us things that you want us to see.

Rain of the future and Rain of the past,

fill me with joy in the path of your steps.

End my journeying; bring me home at last.

I sat in the sun and saw life spread before me,

Day after day turning and turning.

And I knew that on the way I must go

I would be endlessly yearning

For the beauties of yesteryear

lost in the snow.

Life is a tragedy fraught with danger

so hard and difficult none can know.

Show me the way through the endless burning

that leads to a future seeming to glow.

I love the flowers and the grass

which step into the world and pass.

I saw the mirror in the glass

and all the vibrating surrounding life.

I could have forgot it if I tried

but gazed on it and lost my life.

How easily said; how easily done.

We don't remember what we said.

The lies of yesteryear come back to haunt us

and tell us we have lost our life.

I do not wish to think on that,

but blotting it out is far too hard.

The knife into the wound is set

and will not come out without a life.

Do not remember me

when I am gone.

But keep a cherished kiss

from times that were

And all the times that have gone amiss.

Am I a being, trustworthy and free,

made by a God who cares for me?

Or, am I a scion of a long-lost race

that comes from eternity

and has not found its place?

Praise God

Who makes all things well

and did for me

what would forever tell!

Your work is lasting

as clear as the day.

Its result is unending

and lasts to this day.

I opened my heart to our great Creator

who always has me on his mind.

He understood all my ways and creations.

And all that I did was approved in his mind.

He is the Lord who knows a way through

even into the darkest of minds.

What He wants to do, He will accomplish

And save us forever by his great mind.

CPSIA information can be obtained
at www.ICGtesting.com
Printed in the USA
LVHW070330071118
596074LV00001B/1/P